T0290492

Because a Woman's Heart is Like a Needle at the Bottom of the Ocean

Because a
Woman's Heart
is Like a
Needle at
the Bottom of
the Ocean

Sugar
Magnolia
Wilson

AUCKLAND
UNIVERSITY
PRESS

For Mum & Dad,
Harland & Delphi

First published 2019
Reprinted 2019
Auckland University Press
University of Auckland
Private Bag 92019
Auckland 1142
New Zealand
www.press.auckland.ac.nz

© Sugar Magnolia Wilson, 2019

ISBN 978 186940 890 9

Published with the assistance of Creative New Zealand

A catalogue record for this book is available from the National Library of New Zealand

Book design: Katrina Duncan
Cover design: Keely O'Shannessy

Printed in New Zealand by Ligare

Contents

Dear sister

I write to you this morning from my desk overlooking the garden.
I can see Toby clearing grass from beside the path where I walked
earlier. The way my shoes crunch upon the white pebbles of the path,
I find it pleases me. There is something about our clothes, the taffeta,
silks, stitched leather of our shoes, the sounds they make against the
world, brushing upon things, rustling. I wonder if any person from
the past or the future has thought or will think the same: *Oh, I like the
way this stiff linen cuff feels brushing against the paper as I write*, or, *I love
the sound of mother's shoes clicking on the cool stones of the passageway.*

This morning the sun rose like jewellery, only so much more than
jewellery and less of that lonely feeling that gifts of precious stones
and metals give me. What is it with men and things – here is this little
coloured chunk of earth, stick it to your finger and now give me your
person, your selfhood, your body, all the hours of the rest of your
days. My heart belongs to mornings like this one. It was my own.
The world was still but alive, and I could hear men in the distance
beginning to husband their animals. A faraway dog was barking;
somewhere, someone was calling out to her children.

Dear sister

Today I have decided to write to you as if I were a man. Dear sweet sister of mine. Today I took a walk to the local store and I took my beagle with me. His hair is greying and his gait uneven and he is slow. He was on a long leather leash and the morning sun flickered off his eyes, which shone pale and fiery. The air was bracing and so I took many healthful deep breaths, slow and repeated, until I felt like a great train carrying a cargo of personal industry forward into the future. As I puffed and chugged my way along the country path to the store, my tune became: *I shall make the future brighter, I shall make the future brighter, I shall make the future brighter*. My plumes of breath, that were really smoke, rose up and up until the whole world and the surrounding lands were covered in my grease and grime; to run my finger down any tree trunk or barn wall or stone fence brought the tip of my finger back as if I'd plunged it right into the heart of darkness.

And I had ruined the world. And so, my dear sweet sister, although I am myself a man, I have come to the conclusion that first, men are terrible, and second, they will ruin absolutely everything.
P.S. – He whose name will never cross my lips again is a hound and I wish he would be hanged.

Dear sister

I am so tired today. Small birds that I am sure belong on dune slopes near the ocean keep circling above our land. They start out near the river and I can only see a faint shape moving in the sky, but they wheel closer and hang like a single feathered lung over our house, inhaling and exhaling. Maybe it is the lung of our family, maybe they sense us, and like a painter at work, their shapes are a natural representation of our familial disparate togetherness. The birds are our collective spirit rendered as a portrait by nature. Or, maybe I am just tired and bored.

Life can be so boring. Have you noticed this? This is when my brain turns faster, the water pushing against the paddles of my waterwheel, and I am sewing and tending and harvesting crops that no one has need for. I am hungry, but cannot eat my own produce, because why would I? What taste would it give me that I do not already know so well? What thing would it bring to me that, if I were a god, I could not already create, knowing every tiny symbol and equation that had to exist in this specific arrangement of factors; I could click my fingers and this thing would be so. Exactly. Again and again, over and over. OH LIFE! Tell me something interesting, sweet sister! Fuel me with otherness, strangeness, filth. Tell me about a time when you were down on your knees, acting outside of your nature. Tell me you are not really my sister.

Dear sister

I have been gifted a horse by Elizabeth and Ernest (I have decided not to use familial pleasantries anymore). I haven't ridden her yet because I haven't been to see her although she has been here for a week now. She stands out in the East Field and I watch her from my room. She is a landscape of muscle and curve, a continent upon which the shadows of clouds pass. Sometimes she appears coal-coloured and stormy-skinned, her flanks rocky and strange in that way that nature is indifferent and strange. Sometimes she stands beneath the oak and is dappled in the gentlest part of spring – her legs sighing their length to the ground, her mane and tail lifting a little at the edges in the warm wind. My urge to run to her is strong, and to push my face deep into the places where her muscles join; to soak up the scent of animal ripeness. But I don't.

I think the theory presented here by this gifted horse is: you can't take the wild from the heart of the girl, but maybe you can put the wild girl upon a horse and teach her to master some of her own terrible hysteria. I am expected to ride her and learn to hold my tongue. But really, she is a strange letter with a heartbeat asking me not to be myself.

A horse will not be my salvation, and so I will not name her.

Dear sister

I have been thinking of you a lot lately and saying your name to myself without knowing I have said it aloud. I keep dreaming about you – that you are just behind me or next to me just out of sight, and I am telling you something sisterly that is both small and trivial but so very important all at once: you understand the strange nuance of my dream sentiment perfectly. When I wake I am momentarily confused as to where you have gone and then saddened to realise that your presence has been a figment of my night mind. In my dreams, you smell as you do in life – of violet water and the leather from riding. I like to sit in the early morning, after these dreams, out on my window ledge and look out over the fields and imagine you cresting the hill on your horse and moving quickly toward the house. Lately, I have been thinking a lot about place, about the notion of home and how it is so often women who are taken from their place.

Everything here on this land has nurtured us. My blood is red from the beet harvest and the rambling rose, my spine made thick and strong from the thatch work of jasmine weaving its riot across our fences – my heart beats with the metre of the newborn pansy greeting the sun for the very first time. This land was our nursery. We were tended and scolded by the river, supported by and thrown from the trees, and birds sang to us in the night when we could not sleep for the unseen things in the shadowed corners of this great, lonely house. Yet, like many women you have been uprooted and planted in foreign soil, your roots growing down into inhospitable layers. I hear word your mother-in-law is as empty as a long-forgotten crypt, and your husband, well, let us say you've had horses who have shown you more of a romantic interest. I wonder, dear sister, are you lost? Can you find your way home?

Dear sister

I have named the horse. She is Lilith.

Dear sister

We ride a lot at night. I slip down the long hallway, my feet bare
and breath shallow, my blood beating hard at my temples. Down
and down the path to the stables past the usual accoutrements of day
– the rake, the barrow – that at night whisper about their shadow-
selves. The night is a strange tune. Past the hustle of elm, and there
she is, Lilith, far from the Red Sea, a night creature without capacity
for fear. A breeder of demons? No. She gives me strength. We ride
out fast and I hear someone out there, some trickster, some two-faced
she-Pan, deep in the forest luring me, daring me. Her voice appears
as those of the songsters: corncrakes, nightjars, the reed and the sedge
warbler, and it takes a different kind of listening to hear the way.
And we hunt for her, furiously, Lilith and I, but we are home, stabled
and in bed before the new day reminds the robin and the redstart
they exist. It's a secret work we do.

Dear sister

There is a road that veers left off the main road north, that you can find with a pinch of luck, under a balsamic moon, when your desire and will for transmutation is strong. You ride for several hours along the road, and at a point that later when you recount your experience you will not remember, the road goes up from the land and into the low-lying October clouds and on into autumn's deepest silence (it is the inverse season in this place).

Beyond is a town you will know very well. There are many familiar things here. The clouds crowd around as if they are the walls of a valley, creating the illusion that there are mountains on the ceiling of the world. It is a disorienting place where everything appears as a mirror. There is a woman waiting for you at the centre of the town square; her palms are cupped and something burns there. This is something for you to consider, dear sister, should you need to leave.

Dear sister

There are many books of maps in our house. Is this something you ever noticed? It strikes me as strange. How did they get here? They are everywhere, some in plain sight and some disguised within the texts of other books. One map book bears no azimuth, no marshland or meridian, but is a map of ancient language. She says:

Tonight I've watched

the moon and then

the Pleiades

go down

The night is now

half-gone; youth

goes; I am

in bed alone

And it is clear to me. Is it not to you? No dallying. Do not waste your time: make haste. Set out before midnight arrives or it will be too late. You (I) must know where Taurus lies, so track your eyes a little to its left and follow the burning constellation, the starred horn of the bull, across the land, and it is there that you will find what you are looking for. Our lost selves. A flame between two cupped hands.

Anne Boleyn

Anne Boleyn had reptilian creatures
dwelling in her ovaries eating
all her eggs.

Henry's sperm, dumb and excited,
would swim in and chomp, chomp
be devoured in seconds, a

16th-century version of *Fear Factor*
in which none of the contenders are
scared of anything at all,

even eating their partner's babies
or chopping off their concubine's
extremities.

She would have chewed the top
off Mary's head

would have gnawed right through
the skull, and if straws had
been invented, sipped
the welling blood till only
the brain was left – an ice cream
ball at the bottom of a berry
sundae.

Then time for the
razor-edged spoon, used
with the Luciferic skill of the
fifth finger.

Anne stood in the corner
of a room hung with velvet –

the plush right angles
a private screen on which
her mind could blossom
darkly outward

with her clever back to men – gasping
anemones left high and dry without
the pandering feminine waters
anywhere around.

There would be no
mollification.

Her back, a straight and
soundless bell chiming its
judgement,

premeditated and
whip-raw with disrespect.

She had the claw marks of
past lives –

the mauling scars of
cold-blooded marauding.

She came out of the
primordial swamp straight into
the mind of humanity,
learned like lightning,

laced her speech with the
stenchless worm of arsenic,
its small and ruthless mouth
attaching to the most tender
place in men and women.

The proof: Catherine's heart – a
hoar-frosted garden, small teeth marks
across its surface, the roots of
anger finally withered and dry.

Anne glimmered coolly –
a magnificent ice axe,
cleaving the earth's breast.

Her shoes the shape of
inbred alligators

squashed the weakest fruit to
rot beneath the pale English sun.

The monster

Frankenstein's monster was
born to peer at his assembled
humanity or lack of
in a world whose water had
turned to ice upon his arrival.

Think: a water spider pushes from
its silked egg only to find the pulse
of the earth turned cold.

Its whittle-tipped legs slip and
slide on the mirrored surface which

shows the many-limbed creature
its own lurching darkness –

says, *Here you are, horrible collection.*

And it wasn't that he
couldn't love; he had
four dead babies crammed
into each eye socket –

like any child who longs
to care for a lost chick but
loves it to death instead.

If he had been able to
touch something gently
he might have kissed the
soft curve of someone's mouth but

with one hand a virgin's
couth paw, the other
an executioner's ironic fist

and with a cock made from the
thick and greening arm of a
19th-century wrestler

what hope had he of
even a simple embrace?

Yet despite the body was his mind –
a rich nebula,
an endless alchemical rotation
amongst the silent stars

he said, *I am the Adam of your
labours*

this is what you've made,

please look at me

and there was a chance, for
just a moment, to peer
into the cool crust of the earth at
ourselves

to get behind that
ashen pack of huskies and
travel with him

beyond.

But no one looked

and he moved away
into the phantom ice
and now we cannot find him.

Betty as a boy

Your New Zealand mother and American stepfather wanted boys,
and that is why, you think, you and your closest sister, the one you are
not related to at all, dressed like Annie Hall. The patterned scarf,
textured tweed, taupe-hued tailoring over mannish knitwear,
a waistcoat and tie.

You and she together, the endlessness of the Oldsmobile, the long
blue motels of the Southwest, sharing beds that creaked with the gravity
of a thousand whispering bodies, building a family between the two of you while
only metres away in the double bed, your mother was just another young woman
joining herself to anger.

You were never the favourite; you were the sad one from the old life,
the needy one who crawled into the shower with your mother, longing
so hard to be loved that she couldn't take it anymore, and punched you,
nine years old, square in your soft desperate face.

Now, your sister, the one you're not related to at all, lives in the hills of California,
in an austere house surrounded by thirsty cacti: prickly pear, barbary fig, parodia,
saguaro, with her ex-jock husband, and you in the Far North of New Zealand,
on a rocky outcrop over the silver Pacific, alone.

Your American and New Zealand lives seem to have calibrated into
expected rhythms: she pressing organic oranges into an elixir, you
with a salty chardonnay; she yoga and you ocean.

But at night your sister places her neat body down in the long,
cool shadow of the saguaro, and sews together the eyes of a lizard with a
cactus spine and spider's silk as thread. In her waking life, so Californian,
tan and usual, at night, like all of us – fragmented and orbiting herself
like a stranger.

She's read too much Carlos Castaneda, smuggled too many boat loads of
drugs from Colombia to Santa Cruz, taken too much peyote to be your
average dream girl with a rearranged nose. She knows cacti like a
cheerleader knows the lonely hours waiting on the inside of a letter jacket.
But she knows that too.

And you, outside the upmarket grocer's, camouflaged top, khaki pants slashed
with a silk of red, a backpack strung with things that clink,
disappearing into your androgyny – the inverse of a newly minted drag queen,
appearing like a flaming comet, burning to be noticed.

Newton Gully mix tape

Auckland, the 80s, parents high
and drinking Daniel Le Brun in
the old state house under the motorway
overpass

the place where a young boy finds an
old balloon in the gutter and tries
to blow it up, the transgression of innocent
breath into the grit-lit corners of
someone else's used-up life

and inside his stepfather is
giving his mother a gift of fancy black lingerie

the muddy incense of expensive
perfume – a good approximation of a
cherry blossom reaching its arm through an open
window on a spring night in Paris
only here, in the cut-rate Babel of
the South Pacific, there are hints of hot
tarmac and frangipani, too.

'Find a fat friend' is the party mantra
for a time when the doctor will still
hand out speed to anyone who knows its trade name,
he'll even turn up to your parents' party wearing
Comme des Garçons, talking in long vowels
and dance with your mother who he's been
secretly in love with for years.

Your father
won't even mind.

Don't forget, the world is almost
still young, the elephants
of the mind still roam in huge,
populous hoards, the *Rainbow Warrior* has
only just stopped floating among the
confetti of floral islands, and we're
angry with the French like a
young woman is angry with her
insouciant lover,

and here, in this city in the summer
the new buildings rising up
are the symptom of the malady, of the
olive-fingered men and their
laidback urban eloquence.

Everyone is slick and fast
even if they're sad.

And in the long grass between
closely stitched houses, a collection of children has
gathered like a bright halo around a fallen thing – a baby bird

they meditate upon the best way to lift it up, to
send it back home, they understand
homesickness, the way it zeroes to your bones,
so the balloon, it's found again and tied around the
delicate body of the bird, and thrown repeatedly up and up and
up into a sky that won't
take it back.

Conversation with my boyfriend

English into 한글

We eat small fish with button eyes from plastic mass graves but
to bite them is so satisfying especially hearing the tiny bones pop
between your gorgeous white teeth. The way you use chopsticks to
harpoon candied potatoes, your symmetric lips deftly consuming
pickled walnuts. I envy the way your heart munches deeply.

In the evening we kiss and your mouth has bloomed into a sour
flower but I don't mind. You call me Flower-Piglet and when you do
I call you Tiger and see us both flying over the city like two super
animals.

You are always full of rice because you eat rice and you love rice and
your skin feels like rice when we hug – our bodies mould together
and we are a bread yin and a rice yang and although traditionally
Korean people don't eat bread you are more than hungry to have me.

Sleeping, you dream of a field of red cabbages. I am in the long dry
lines between the rows wearing wooden sandals and talking with your
mother who speaks to me in circles and squares, which I use to cut
and gather crisp leaves into urns.

But when you wake I have brown eyes and you still call your own
eyes black even though that is impossible and when I cook rice it just
doesn't seem to hold. And, you speak quietly in Korean when you call
your mother. And, you say, *Shhh, don't speak*, when your father calls.

한글 into English

We enjoy the ocean's yield in the same container, small fish with
a slim eye beaded through the skull, seeing themselves in salted
bunches. You try to lasso wild rice from the bowl and watch my
brave teeth doing natural things.

We kiss and your lips are fluent with sugar, and it is nice but salt is
an important part of any meal. I call you Flower-Piglet because I do
not call you all the time, even when you call me. You say we are two
small animals like pigs flying over the city to see our way into the
evening and I say, *Which city? Where?*

We should always be filled with rice: cooking it and eating meals
together, and rice is important before we die, too. We hug and your
skin is learning to love rice, or, at least starting to star the healthy
map of rice. Traditionally, Korean people don't eat bread, but there
are now many patisseries in larger cities, and many children long to
be pastry chefs, and I am not so sure about this.

In sleep, I dream of the red cabbage fields, discarded urns, and you
cutting my mother's spicy talk and hanging it on long drying lines
between the rows of vegetables. You bend down to supplant the
cabbages with small strawberry plants.

In the morning, I still have black eyes, but when you wake it seems
impossible to you because eyes cannot be darker than brown.
And when my family calls, you curl silent into the bed sheets like a
flower-piglet resting in the hay and sleep. My 꽃돼지.

Bathhouse night chat

My up-to-ears beard and reindeer jersey is
very handsome and in your winter boots
you look more like a distant, snowy mountain than
a girl who threw on my long coat – but nonetheless
it is very cute.

It is so wintery, and I say, *Take a chance with a*
cleansing bathhouse on the edge of the ocean.
We will wash in separate baths but
sleep in the same room by night,
our heads on wooden pillows;
on the floor we sleep without mats,
just with our body's bones because our
flesh is soft and young.

Drunken men and women come
inside to sleep from under the hard, black sky.
One old woman steals the sleeping block from beneath your head,
and it sounds almost like a ripe and seed-filled
vegetable hitting the floor.

So I tell you, *Pumpkin is a nickname for an ugly woman in*
South Korea, but I do not understand your
sudden shock.

It is not a matter of feminism!

I might say cutie if she's just right or flower-piglet
if I am deeply in love, but an ugly woman?
If she's growing in long orange lines
under the sun even she will say,
Yeah, you found me down on the farm.
Even she will admit to this.

Korean women are strong and honest.
This is what you fail to grab.

But it's not you, don't worry, and I don't have a small face, either.
I want to be a model, but in Korea it's not attractive,
this variety of big-sized head.
To cut down the bones of one's face is a
possibility, and if I save enough money
I might manage surgery.

So, sleeping here with you on the planks and
your head bouncing against the floor like that,

I am grateful not to hear the rattle of
a thousand golden seeds.

Home Alone 2 (with you)

Christmas time and we've been out all night.
You've been speaking a mix of Korean and English,
the way you do when you're drunk – and
because English is your second language
people can't be sure if you're
talking over their heads or if
you're freestyling your own
kind of poetry.

I think it's the best thing ever.

Finally, we make it home, settle our tired selves
on the hot mat and turn on the TV.

It's *Home Alone 2*.
I'm all upbeat and hyped and
doing little air-punching movements
because we're in love and you're
very good-looking and *Home Alone 2* is on and
there is nothing better I could imagine
watching right now.

Kevin McCallister is already going through
the character-defining section
of his trials and tribulations by the time
we tune in – his blonde locks lapping like
pure shine around his pink exclamation-
marked face.

You're moving around the room doing the things
that you do – putting on house shorts and
a singlet, rolling around on the mat, talking
to yourself.

The baddies are really just a device to help
Kevin and his family realise how much they
mean to one another, I say. *His absence*
is what hurts but matters the most.
It's a coming of age story.
It's a love story.

The movie goes on and I get really involved –
I forget you're there.

Kevin is over it. He's lonely to the point of
despair. He misses his mother. He goes to
the Rockefeller Christmas tree and prays for
only one thing, to see her again. And then there
she is, calling his name.

And this is when my heart finally knows
what my mind has for years – that I won't
ever find a tree laced bright enough with
festive lights to guide my own mother through
the city streets. There are no streets that
connect our separate worlds.

And I turn around and realise you've been
watching me the whole time – and even
though neither of us have spoken and I've
not started to cry yet you say really quietly,
Do you miss your mother?

And I am so startled, and so shockingly sad that
I cry in front of you for the first time. I cry
on you for what seems like hours and
your white top feels like home
and for a while you let me be a kid again,

a kid who got lost and can't seem to
find her mother anywhere,
no matter how hard she looks.

Full moon celebrations

We are at your parents' house
for Seollal.

A solar system of side dishes spins
out on the table, each one
neat and small, dazzling me with
their individual medicinal properties.

The chicken soup to
salt and bind the
fraying web of my
heart

the kimchi to
braven my voice

the octopus to
leak its inky pupils
into my brain,
marinating it for
serious thought.

All these things handmade as though
wrought from the empty air of the kitchen
into something-ness.

You set out waxen quarters of
potato like prayer candles

sprouts that bask on
supple vertebrae

sliced tongues of white radish
lapping in their own
sour waters.

All of these things fill
the shallow bowls until there is
enough to light up the waning
space between us.

Heat wave

There were deep yellows between the blue bars of night.
We moved among them easily as the summer licked
our skins to a high gloss.

You dragged me down laneways, bought me a
ruby necklace that looked like a drop of blood at my throat.

In the jewellery shop a bright pink bird drowsed on a branch.
I stroked its tiny closed eyes with the back of my tiger-print
fingernail, enclosed the warm body in my hand.

She is sick, said the shop assistant,
flapping her lashes, factually.

The bird opened its eyes, stared at me with the most
tender of intimacies, and closed them again.
I looked to you, moved, but you had your back to me, humming
a K-Pop tune, playing with dream catchers in the shop window.

We walked up the hill to the street where small carts sold
cocktails in plastic pouches, drank two Long Island Iced Teas
for our fried-egg brains and ambled the endless warren of streets.

I petted a purple octopus waving in a bowl, told you I thought it was
likely octopuses were my spirit animal and you laughed, kissed my eyes,
*Not special! Delicious. It's not your spirit animal. It was your dinner animal,
just last night.*

We battled our way home, valiant in our drunkenness as
men waved radishes in our faces and old women elbowed our sides
and the moon was just another grubby lamp on a
night-coloured pole.

We slept long into the next hot day,
one of us a love-sick bird, opening heavy lids to stare.

Snow chart

It is snowing for the first time in twenty years.
Millions of iced flowers are falling from the sky.
But love is just another way of looking at the weather, I think.
We are on my bed and you have a piece of paper and a pen.
You are drawing a graph to show me how love changes
over time.
Two small people with rough biro bodies and big heads
walk along the x-axis, holding hands.
They are you and I heading into our own future.
It can be tough to walk through love, you tell me gravely.
The y-axis charts the push and swell of your feelings,
starting low the days after we met at the club and then
creeping up. Come now, our second winter, and the line rockets skyward.
You wave the paper at me. *See? Did you see that?*
This is how much I love you now.
I nod. We both look out the window, where the
snow has covered everything.

The moon and my 'house':
A review of Haruki Murakami's novel, *1Q84*

There is an electronic moon attached to the side of my 'house'. It emits a low hum and is neon white. It might sound funny but it's not. At night when I have the blinds pulled to an appropriately 70s-cop-interrogation-room angle, the iced light scans across my body and I feel like nothing but a collection of meaty braille being read by an indifferent finger.

In these moments, I am sure I am the calm-in-the-face-of-sheer-madness protagonist of a Haruki Murakami novel – yet to realise her massive inherent power; yet to realise her breasts are perky and perfectly shaped like small Mt Fujis shining brightly in the sun; yet to realise the other half of the universe is some shy math teacher with a natural six-pack.

Beneath this indifference I feel like a glistening, wet creature. But it is more apt to say that I feel less like any living thing than I do a state. I am a voiceless want. An ache on the sheets. Maybe the metaphor of a sprig of something organic in a shadowy place frequented only by slightly magical cats, pushing its way up toward a pinprick of light far above – whether it's a star or the exit outta here, the sprig never knows.

At the end of a Haruki Murakami novel we are not sure if we are sure or not. There seems to be a form of resolution but we were never clear in the first place which side of the door represented internal or external reality. And in some way this huge planetary wing mirror attached to my 'house' pushes me further into and further out of the world.

The space in my room breathes and on the exhale it bends everything including my body and yet-to-be-realised perfect breasts in a convex sheet out toward the soupy night. I do not know where my internal organs end and where the neon street sign begins, but it doesn't matter – it's all sexy. All red. All ruby. All wet. All glistening. All some kind of entrance or exit.

Pup art

We are in the backyard and you
have thrown my dog into the sky –
she levitates somewhere over the
neighbour's house; she is a long-haired
Golden Retriever, and she catches the sun full whack
and shines hot like a star.

Before she floats any higher you
hurl a net over her body, peg
the twine taut to the lawn
so she is suspended against
the pull of space.

– *THIS IS ART!* – you proclaim

your arms goalposts through
which only silence flies.

We all gaze up at my dog –
her face peaceful as she banks and
rolls forward.

Oh! someone gasps, *she's like the*
slow kid in gym class! Her gold threads
tangling with the net, her nose
lifting a little as though she smells cat
on the wind.

Pull her down! I cry,
she's just a little animal – she is
not art she is so soft round the
edges – so tender at the centre.

But she is going, the peg hooved
from the ground, the blue-town-sky
holding her up.

She whistles a little, a
small halo of mutt round her
nose, the long net a robe
sailing out behind her
as she moves off over the roofs
without once looking back
so yellow –

just that bit more
defined against the pure blue
than the rest of us.

Final 8os exposé

At an auction of Jacqueline Fahey's art
all your old teachers in their
batik headbands drink Henkell Trocken

and swing parrot earrings from
pulled lobes.

Every face is almost the one
you want to see and
every conversation about a
daughter that isn't quite you –

she's an awfully clever scholar

she's beautiful at science

and her algebra is simply

magnifique

On the floor a river of peewees,
clinkers and galaxies roll in a
stream toward a small hole in the corner
of the room

and children scrabble about on
their knees dragging collaged
party hats behind them like
parachutes.

From downstairs there is

a rhythmic thump

        thump

        thump

where a Morrissey concert
that you're dying to get to has
already begun but

the auction hasn't started yet
and you're fretting because you
need to get away and because
you need *that* painting,

the one where your mother,
finished teaching for the day,
sits at a table
her diamond rings hazed in
Pall Mall smoke

and the wispy brown
quarter moon of a
child's head can be
seen to rest against
her knees.

Glamour

dedicated to bowerbirds and the lovelorn everywhere

I have seen some put down soft materials – ferns,
leaves and vine tendrils for no one. Some placed sticks
around loose foundations like a bracken crown
and built little roofs that sagged but
didn't let the rain in.

Others had pomegranate seeds littered
across the dust and others still,
flints of yellowing bone.

Often, they waited days, filled their time
collecting shells, nuts, flowers, feathers,
seeds, stones and berries. Discarded pegs, caps,
coins, bullets, clips, pins and glass.

There was a lot of lonely dancing.

Others collected sounds instead – imitated the
local pigs, waterfalls and chatter. They ran round clowning,
hooting like self-assured owls.

But, sometimes nothing works.

Finally, sick of the endless effort
some of them gave up on waiting
and pulled unwilling girls
right out of the sky, took them home.
One girl tasted the walls with her
triangular tongue – the cheap taste of
ditchwater and decaying twigs –

resigned herself to her fate.

Another stared at her own reflection in the
wall of beetles' backs, felt a hunger for
something she'd never have.

Moon-baller

Open up your mouth and
we'll press our lives together.

In the future you'll stop breathing,
and in a loving way we either will
or will not have been kind enough
to each other in this lifetime.

Remember the night we thought
we heard an owl telling the future?

Remember, no matter how hard
we looked, we couldn't find its
two pale orbs among the camellia's
thatched branches.

What I meant that night but
said badly, or didn't say at all was:
your b-baller's touch was
like a stone fruit – hot from the sun,
tender, but with an aftertaste
of rocky indifference – traces of planet,
mineral, amethyst, a hint of dry river bed.

I think I am terrified of being
left alone with a spade on a
small, sweet-skinned moon where
the view is beautiful but
nothing will grow.

So, I'll kiss you on your
big pink mouth, but leave before
I learn it's me who's not fit
for life.

Spent

The night sky is full of
  stars but

we are more clever than
most – we know
they are just
        burned bones.

Nothing beautiful –

not space sailors blown
from their ships – the light from
treasure quickly grasped
in their fists

only reaching us now.

It's a useless kind of light –
    unspendable.

The palm of your hand lies
on my knee
            like a gold coin
        donation

trying to free up my joints

but I don't feel like
    moving
        or shining.

And your voice has had
its heartwood cut out

a woodpecker taps a hollow
sound against
the bark casing where

other things dwell
now – rats and
stoats, wide-mouthed
egg-swallowers too.

In the dark your face
is different – you have more
teeth than normal and
                    your mouth

looks expensive.

Gingerly

I dream you have a life
you've never told me about.
That what I know of you is like
a cloud-striped crystal viewed in the
gap between tall apartment blocks.
It's the same colour as the weather.

That you have a chestnut horse
with clean white socks who steps
gingerly from her stable onto frosty grass
in the mornings and she doesn't like
the snow. There are surrounding
mountains like bells of glass.

This is where you and your family
have moved – to a large, wild patch
of land somewhere in a
neighbouring dimension but
with roads that never quite
cross paths.
And you didn't tell me.

That your wife graduated
with first class honours from
art school, that she's exhibited
many times.

That she bends over to wipe
your baby's mouth. And I can see
her pink underwear rise up
beneath her jeans – they're an old pair, a
when-everything-else-is-in-the-wash pair –
and when she turns around with the
dirty cloth to look at me, her face is
identical to mine.

Spirit-liver

Every single one is born with a formation – sometimes
more than one. It's considered unlucky if it's visible but
at least the world will only be cruel to you in a plain way.

Some of the formations grow like a mermaid's purse in an
opaque corner of the sea. They're worn in a quiet place,
the scales soft and sea-soaked so they are like petals to the touch –
they replicate over and over until there is a three-dimensional relief
and an object exists.

They are worn on the lungs. The bones, etc.
On the heart it's like a letter written in invisible ink,
a tale told in secret over and over, so many times
that the mind starts to believe it.

That's how illness starts.[1]

A secret message carried through the cells until the cells cannot
cancel the noise. Change is informed by persistence.
Like a rock licked by water so many times it forgets what it's like
to feel like a rock – plain and simple and sun-struck.

The water licks at so many things, carries tiny bits
of the licked thing away until, in a thousand years, the
licked thing dissolves like bread.

That's what happened to the man I used to love. He went to work
on a farm in the Coromandel and one day he wandered off
into the bush and he got lost and couldn't find his way back.

He said he wouldn't have died from starvation or dehydration, but
from the shame of it all. A buzzing heat wave of stupidity.
A conched shell of calcium spiralling up to strangle the air.

---

1   That's what stupid people say.

He arrived back from his trip to tell me and I hated him for it.

My ex, he wore his formation on his spirit-liver.
That's not the liver that lurks in your body, but the shadow-liver
that lives a foot to the right of the real thing, attached by a soft string.

The spirit-liver helps to clear away the things we
poison ourselves with: people who talk more than
they listen, intrusive mothers, pretend introverts,
non-flexi workplaces.

And so he still lived with his mother at 26 and his father
never knew how to shut up. And the beer in him.
It kept sloshing away at his actual liver until the cells couldn't block
out the sound of, *I'm lost, I'm lost, I'm lost.*

But he wasn't ill, just adrift somewhere.

The man I love now hides his in his left fibula. It
is the bone of accelerating a car fast enough to clear
a cliff and slo-mo into the sea, and it is the bone of pushing off the
edge of a building strong enough to clear any obstruction.

He wears the sorrow of his father and his brother down there,
holding them tight in the warmth of his marrow.

Cabin

All of time played out before we left the house. Two internal suns
the only light, slipping through the door to the feet of tall pines.
I said I liked who you were turning out to be, and that was strange
considering it was my own hair caught in the tallest boughs, my
hipbones in the reeds, ankles littered everywhere – all of them
attracting piles of white stones and a pocket's worth of small birds.
You filmed us in the house having sex for 'anthropological purposes'.
We were the one mammalian warmth in the whole cold forest. We lit
the cabin up like a lantern and things were attracted to the sweet
glow. I whispered, *Narrate like you know our behaviour's results*, and the
pines bent to look in through the windows, the cones opened their
many wings, and sighing, let the night reach deeper. We were both
human and this seemed enough.

Because a woman's heart is like a needle at the bottom of the ocean

When we have sex and I can't see your face and your hair is tied up, I feel
like I am having sex with myself or myself as yourself. I am a good boyfriend.
I am emotionally stable but in the bedroom I dominate in a gentle fashion.
I am blonde and brunette and I wear both of my head hairs up in a topknot.
Sometimes I whisper to myself in Mandarin – I say there's no 我 in 队,[1] and the
small mountains inside me burn. The forests sway a little. And there is possibly
someone who comes out of a tiny cabin in a valley and yells something inaudible
but meaningful up the slopes toward us. I cannot hear her well, did she say,
什么都没有意思了, 但一切都是非常非常重要的?[2] And somewhere a yang
moon is speaking about a job she just applied for while a man who feels just
like me appears to be listening but is thinking about what he wants to say next.
The night crosses its leg over the day and the ankles don't touch in the middle
because 女人心海底针.[3]

---

1   There's no I in TEAM.
2   Nothing means anything at all, but everything is so very important.
3   A woman's heart is like a needle at the bottom of the ocean.

Crane fly

She has common objects there –
a blanket, only necessary bowls, some eating utensils. Things are
simpler and things are done with much gravity.
There are rituals, common rituals that involve
body and water and stone. Cleaning. Drinking. Being still.
When I visit my mother, she is a transparent crane fly. The house is so beautiful.
There is cleared land and a fence beyond where there are fields with wildflowers and
this is bordered by rows of tall trees. Poplar.
She is a crane fly. A crane fly.

Mother

Mothers contain fertile silence. They emerge from shapeless gentleness into textured gentleness, and often mate with portions of this abstract materiality. Mothers search for mates by walking great distances or sometimes flying. The connection of fertile silence with abstract materiality takes a few minutes and may be accomplished in flight.

Mothers are therianthropic and have a lifespan of 100 days after which they dig their bodies down into wet soil or beds of algae and emerge hours later in familiar but untouchable forms. Once reborn, mothers lay their realised gentlenesses onto the surface of a domestic water body or into the corner of a white room, and some simply drop them in flight, their inherent sensory faculties allowing them to measure where the wind will carry their young.

Most eggs will be isolated. The surface of each egg has a crack which channels light out into the darkened world. This light may help to anchor the newborn to the empty room into which it arrives.

The lake has a long memory

There were lights here last night
charging up the dark matter between us
and the water and the water
and its sister, the sky.

It is impossible to touch you.

I don't know who said this – it was either
you or me or somebody's drowned
childhood friend, lost and lost and
lonely forever on the bottom of the
bottom of the lake.

Somebody told me there is no
bottom to this lake. That the water just
goes down goes down and down forever.

The lake has a long memory a long
memory, a large imagination.

When my mother left the spring
on our land didn't change. The water didn't
stop didn't stop bubbling up from below.
It didn't cover itself in a shawl of blackbirds
to indicate grief.

Each litre of water that came up
was different from the next and the next
and each time and each time after that
when I took a drink a drink I became
a deep blue lantern teeming with invisible life.

Nobody had gone anywhere at all.
Nobody was ever lost at the bottom
of the lake because in the lake
it is impossible to be a stranger.

Muddy heart

You'll lie down one day on the field behind
your house and your heart will turn
to mud.

Dandelions will push up through the earth, your
blood mingling to a rich beet-coloured soil,
your bones some kind of ash like your father uses
around the strawberry plants.

Clover and pennyroyal will take seed on you.
You'll call out in the fading light for your father,
who is, after all, just over the fence in the house – but you'll
sound like the long grass, the frogs, the dogs herding cattle.
When he eventually comes looking for you,
how ever many years later

there will only be the green flush of land down toward
the road, the river and a patch of grass
where he will tend to sit from now on.

Town

In the small town with
the grey clouds like
quiet dogs

on the veranda with our
feet up watching ghosts
in the old corner garden
where the oleander dips deep

I am myself and not myself
again and again and again
until you find me through
the small water in my wrist

the channel where the darkest
fish run to the lake in my palm.

It is raining.

You hold my arm there, on
the Formica-topped table
with more gravity than a
metal earth

softer than a soft sea.

I am yours driving down and
diving

homing around and around
and back again.

Bone tired

Today the baby sleeps restlessly.

From her crib she hears
the wind rattle
the window frames that
haven't been touched since 1904.

The clothesline loses another
string, neon pegs stud the blue,
the sky full of all the sheets
I once had, all of the pillowcases
I've dreamed upon – my night world lost
to the clear blanch of day.

This wind she will
rattle you apart,

hassle your bones until they
do not remember
their purpose.

My knees are
already tired –
the sweet chemistry of
movement

getting more and more
lost to me with each
climb of the hill each
hoist of the baby each
blast of the northerly.

In the Karori graveyard are all those
dead from the wind and from
hills and babies.

Everything is soft there – the edges of
headstones, the sounds of names:
Delilah, Maude, Henry.

Only a glade of honeysuckle grows
wild and strong because if you
know how to hide
you might live a little longer.

My grandmother, so many silk
scarves gifted to her by her
grandson in Hong Kong,

yanked, stolen, thieved
from her neck and thrown into
the sea at Seatoun –

she gave up, had enough, her bones
turned to dust and she blew away.

I visited the old stone church
where she worshipped:

it was empty,

and I smelled
oranges and coal, and felt
brown parcel paper and string
on my fingertips

and heard the tap of feet that
danced the Highland Fling.

After a trip to Auckland I
met my cousins down at
Seatoun Wharf.

We opened the small tin and
threw her into the sky where
the wind grabbed her
and boomeranged her back
toward us.

But, a small puff of her escaped,
banked left, high above
Peter Jackson's house and
was carried away.

The sleep of trees

I photosynthesise in the half-light
between the curtains
the low vibration of my
                    growth

small boats upon the light
they carry sugars to feed the
birds in my hair and all the
                    whistling

the whistling keeps me awake and
hypnotised.

I am growing but shedding
hosting life and
            dying all at once, I am
           buzzing in the crack between
dusk and dawn and spinning like a

           spent Catherine wheel in the
loamy places beneath the
           lemon tree.

When trees sleep they
           relax their branches
and I

I am trying to relax all of the bones and
so
  is she even though
she is small and you would imagine
naturally
       relaxed but

we are reaching down
        wrist deep in this life and
        turning up to meet our feet with
           the rushing
                with the clouds that do not have time
to pause.

This is what sleep looks like –
           like it is a communion
between us and the
hidden worms the ones
that work at night the ones that
           compost the world's shame –

the ones that try to wend around the
collective dream of
           tin foil the
psychic stain of condoms, the vacuum pack
around the
           meat of our hearts

those ones – deep in the soil
working
    working

so that we
can
rest.

But this is not the sleep of trees this
           is the sleep of

horse and foal, always awake to the tune
of the wolf and with
no choice but

to be in love with the music

this is the sleep of mothers – of
five thousand lit candles burning hot in the
dark hall of the body, eyes open
and flaming over the bars of a cot

the sleep of babies – restless turning
a sweet and angry clock
bending in space as it draws earthward, pushing
out and protesting against
                    the constraints
                        the boredoms
                            the repetitions.

It is the no-sleep of both of us, of the slow
train of our bodies reaching morning
with our cargo of
heat and
        exhaustion, anger and
surrender.

But we are trying
            anyway.

And I think maybe
            it is working because
in the morning I am turned to woodlands, and she

                between her toes – a white blossoming of the hopeful kind
                            is pushing up to greet the sun

and around her the earth
moves.

Dear X

I don't know what to say to the idea that you've been dreaming so vividly about me. I feel spooked by it, not only because I too have been having peculiar dreams about you, but because I feel these dreams of mine have been of your making – that I've been called into your subconscious, into your altered state, and in the vulnerability of sleep I haven't had the ability to protest. I have been silent and acquiescent at my core, my whole being mutely drifting into yours, my ear listening to whatever intangible rites your dream mouth whispers. I am a mere projection.

In these dreams, we go on to do terrible things. We become smoke-veiled mountains that block the sun. We become suns that burn for the sake of burning, and constellations that mislead the weary traveller. I realise these are just dreams, but they feel so real and when I wake I remember that while I love you, I have also always been afraid of you. You are so good in that you've spent your life fighting against your own carnivorous spirit. Yet how easily you eat the yolk of people's confidence! And I know they see that toothy look in your eyes, that ferocity rising up.

In polite company one strange remark from a lady, well, it seems too petty and small for a person to comment upon, to ask someone's true meaning, and so, people leave your company feeling unsettled, wondering if they have misinterpreted you, wondering if it's their own sense of self they need to reflect upon. But you've left them with a rotting seed, a burr stuck fast to their heart they cannot pare off, and they grow to fear you in private, afraid to ask if others feel the same. Slowly, I think, this secret fear becomes awe and from this lack of confrontation I see you grow more powerful.

You are noticed. I hear you talked about in many different circles. People don't know what to say when you are raised as a topic. After your name and the usual wheres and whens, there are often silences and shiftings. Gentlemen sip their drinks and glance about, hoping someone else will offer comment so they don't have to. Ladies will cast a smile too broadly about the circle.

I am not mistaken in saying that your energy, the assembled parts that make up your particular construction, are anomalous. You are an agitating agent to the general sense that 'all is well'. People are waiting to see where you go and what you set yourself upon.

Do not waste your talents or your time. The Pleiades are calling you to action, only not in the woods as you've imagined, but here – at the centre of the new world.

Pen pal

1.

Hellooo. How are you?

I've only just started
witchcraft so this letter
includes some of my hairs.

My two guinea pigs had
million dollar babies –

two lots of babies.

Mum says they have the
eyeless ways of newborns.

Friday and I'm sitting
in the quad under the
acacia tree.

The bell has rung
and I'm waiting for
Mum or Dad to pick me up.

No one has come. It is
strange.

Did I tell you? I owe $1.50 to
the school canteen.

Mum says I don't feed
them often enough but
I do.

My lips are in a terrible way –
they are so fannyish

when I am older they
will droop.

Everything gets older.

With my third eye I sense
my little guinea pigs are
in

some kind of
life-ish trouble.

P.S. Did I tell you

in July a meteorite fell?

Blue flashes in the
field it

still glows in the
rain sometimes.

But that doesn't mean nuffink –
it still sucks shit to
live in the bush.

2.

Important data:

the geese are naked.
I owe $1.50 to the school canteen.
I think I am carrying a grief tree.

It is tiny and luminous.

Yesterday I broke one cutting
from each of Dad's African plants

(he was down by the Para pool
slashing ginger).

Remember, I told you –
I only have one booklet?

It said: *Spell for sadness* –

> *Look for your inner breath.*
> *Into a quiet room take*
> *some clean beeswax and*
> *a selection of branches – mix.*
>
> *On your back – breathe like a*
> *long canoe – let the sadness*
> *wash off your*
> *secret underside.*
>
> *Plant to redden in your*
> *garden.*

I look every day but
I am still waiting.

Meanwhile: there has been
irregular blood on my shorts –

a Japanese doctor had to
feel my fanny.

I have nuffink else to say.

Write soon.

3.

Halleluiah, konnichiwa and
jumbo.

There is a tortoise that has
a broken shell and I
want to climb into the TV
and kiss it on the face.

My guinea pigs ran away –
I was sick of feeding them
anyway – some kind of

horrid relief.

I broke the last of our
bad luck cups – Mum thinks
I smashed it on purpose.
She says I need to
contemplate the importance
of all sentient beings (wha?!).

You have not written.

I think I am cursed with
pen pals – first Dev Kalsha
masturbated on me. And Sky,
she just stopped writing.

4.

This letter is in a terrible way –
knows no end.

She (Mum) is a skellington of
nothingness: shardy bones,
spider webs, a small
tortoise with a broken shell.

I think she must be
afraid of something.

He (Dad) took datura –
searched for herds of dead
sheep, his old dog Gamble
under the beds.

We are in the pitch and swing
of winter – my cat Star is
giving me sly sideways glances from
beside the fire.

She says to tell you:

I am an old soul,
blissful, and
I would like
a little bag of
fantails and some
mayonnaise, please.

Remember: I'm not dead
I'm just stuck in the bush.

5.

I put an ad in the *Northern Age*.
It said,

Attention all female mice:
I am a young male mouse looking for
someone to share my bungalow
with. Approximately one month after
moving in we will be shifting to a
state-of-the-art Sam Mouse House.
If interested please call 4085530.

I've had two calls so far – one from
a man in Ahipara with six
four-month-olds.

I could collect them in
two weeks' time.

The other from this girl Natasha –
she has grime on her neck
every day.

The scabbiness of
the valleys.

The other day in gym class she
was bleeding and I said,

Maybe your stomach ate your
heart and now your fanny
is shitting it out.

(She's kind of fat.)

She cried and I felt
bad.

6.

It said: *Spell for an apology –*

> *Return to your thankfulness as*
> *we all may go blind somewhere*
> *down the road.*

> *The new moon's eyeless ways.*

> *During a yellow October*
> *an old book, a few lavender seeds.*

> *Place between and bring the*
> *palms of paper together.*

> *Kneeling*

> *bury in the woods*
> *beneath the light bounced*
> *off the moon.*

> *Let*

> *your heart glow*
> *so red*
> *when it rains.*

7.

In this envelope –
howling.

She (me – *hello*) is in a be-mean-
to-anything-and-everything mood.

I hate my sister and Dad
and Mum. I told her –

Dying is ornamental
(I read it somewhere).

She looked sad.

I think it's because
Princess Di just died
(hey – that rhymes).

I am sitting at the
upstairs desk and

there is an amethyst
mist spreading up the valley.

Its edges are turning black and
rolling toward our house.

All the flowers in the
garden look like fire spirits

burning out in the
evening sun but

I am still waiting
for the small red tree
in the garden to grow.

No word. From you.
I hate you.

P.S. I'm watching, half hearing
your heart so remember

if you get a boyfriend or
Nike shoes

I'll kill you.
Chop
chop.

8.

Yesterday I carried my grief tree
down to the mailbox
to be milled by a letter –
one from you.

There wasn't anything but
a grape-sized spider waving
its front legs in salutation.

This tiny tree loves me too much.
So warm in the dark,
its roots dig in like
chicken's feet.

It hurts sometimes.

When I got home my dad
touched my forehead – his
chest puffed out

that she will . . .
that her bones . . .
it doesn't mean . . .

I think I am that sad-beautiful
girl from that movie – you
remember?

I would have glasses like two
saucers of milk

speak often of unusual flowers and
their Latin names and have

a boyfriend with violent
brown eyes.

Grass-in-the-wind music would
follow me everywhere.

9.

It said: *Spell for impending loss –*

*Push your canoe out
into the silence, your arms
wide like a water bug.*

*Let the smoke from
your heart rise up
through the pink teepee to
sting your constellations.*

*Cry through a selection of
possible losses:*

*your father's – his wife
yours – your mother
your mother's – her life.*

*Push your boat farther
away from the shore than*

it has ever been.

*Get so lost that nothing is
familiar.*

One day

*try to make it
home again.*

10.

Hi.

Tomorrow Mum goes
to the Mexican clinic.

I feel like a cagey fox in a
field where there are no
delicious babies to eat.

Maybe it's because I am
waiting for dinner – it seems to
take so long these days.

Yesterday Mum crashed the
car. I didn't know till
they drove past me on the road
and stopped.

It was really strange – Mum and
Dad looked like two people
who didn't know me.

You know in the movie how
Sarah and Bud acted when they
first started going round?

Well, a sad version of that,
like it was just
them on the planet.

For a while I felt as if my
head was underwater and
I was looking up at them
through layers of
old branches

or like a boat out and tangled
in the mangroves

getting farther and
farther away.

II.

In my room –
black smoke and the
pages of a book turned

as if the wind had
murmured through but

it hadn't.

Dad says we sometimes
mistake the passing wind for

something calling out.

Yesterday I found one
of my guinea pigs

on the lawn with a
broken back.

Dad and I dug a hole in
the garden and he saw
the branches missing
from his African trees.

He didn't say anything.

Do you think you
have ghosts
in your house?

I am just a little
afraid of the night.

I can hear cats
and trees preen themselves
into humans.

When Renee stayed the night
she said Star called my name
all night long.

Maggie, Maggie.
Tonight a black cricket
is my guardian angel.

12.

Are you dead too?

I haven't heard from
you in so so long.

This is just to say that

the funeral is next
week

and

I wish you could come.

13.

I write to you from
the witching hour.

He is out in the night
calling to his garden –

he is a big-hearted grasshopper
licked over by the long, red
tongue of sadness.

I could hear it all evening – the fridge
saying, *open, close, open, close*
and the cold cheap gush
of cask wine.

Earlier he tried to call me down, said

Maggie, don't be sad!
Come and dance!

and I yelled back

Go be killed by a tree, Dad.

But later, I am like a tree
struck by lightning,

and the only thing
that blossoms is that
scented dream fear –
the night bloom which
attracts night creatures.

Now it is so late and out my
window I can hear him near
the old apple tree.

His hands are in the air and
there is darkness leaking down
his fingers

even though the moon
is big.

There is no one in the
house now but
me and Star . . .

I think.

14.

Star is getting old.
Soon she will be 14.

Dream I had last night:

in the flowering apple tree a little
flash of light and a small bundle,

something wrapped in soft
cloth, fell down.

My afraid-of-the-darkness
seemed to come from outside
of me and welcomed more darkness.

It stunk and made my
body all rickety.

I got to the tree and unfolded
the soft cloth –

a thin-lipped thing, shallow stony eyes,
with her back broken like

an isosceles triangle.

It was Star.

It was so weird 'cause
in my dream I cried the most
emotional cry I've
ever cried –

it felt like a cold black river
I knew well but had
forgotten for so long

had finally found me
again.

And when I woke up my pillow
was soaked right through
and smelt like silt and
wet stones.

15.

It said: *Spell for releasing fear –*

> *Fear flutters in a puddle of*
> *water lilies: transience.*
>
> *Plant a wand of apple tree*
> *into the earth and*
>
> *be patient with the*
> *black seeds glinting so sharp*
> *in your heart*
>
> *one day they will grow*
> *into a tree*
>
> *and you will*
> *take fruit and wood.*
>
> *With grasshoppers on the tips*
> *of your fingers as*
>
> *a salutation of light that*
> *honours the dark –*
>
> *wave your hands.*

Notes

'Dear Sister' references the Lilith of Jewish mythology who refused to become subservient to Adam.

'Dear Sister' uses Sappho's 'Midnight Poem' as translated by Mary Barnard (*Sappho*, University of California Press, 3rd ed., 2012, fragment 64).

'Dear Sister' uses the line 'a flame between two cupped palms' from Margaret Atwood's poem 'Variation on the Word *Sleep*' (*Selected Poems II: 1976–1986*, Houghton Mifflin Company, 1987, 77).

'Final 80s Exposé' uses lyrics from the song 'Algernon's Simply Awfully Good at Algebra' by Malcolm McLaren and the Bootzilla Orchestra (*Waltz Darling*, Epic, 1989, track 7).

'Newton Gully Mix Tape' adapts the line 'and zero at the bone' from Emily Dickinson's poem 'A Narrow Fellow in the Grass' (*The Complete Poems*, Faber & Faber, 2016).

The title 'The Sleep of Trees' is taken from the novel *Special Topics in Calamity Physics* by Marisha Pessl (Penguin Books, 2007).

'Pen Pal' uses some language from the collection *Trances of the Blast* by Mary Ruefle (Wave Books, 2013), although no complete phrases or sentences.

The book's title *Because a Woman's Heart is Like a Needle at the Bottom of the Ocean* is from an ancient Chinese proverb.

'Pen Pal' was first published as a chapbook by Cats and Spaghetti Press in 2014.

Acknowledgements

Thank you to Anna Jackson, without whom this entire book would've taken another ten years to exist. Thank you to Hannah Mettner and Morgan Bach for being the best poetry witch-wives. Thank you to those from all incarnations of our poetry group: Emma Barnes, Zarah Butcher-McGunnigle, Carolyn DeCarlo, Ya-Wen Ho, Anna Jackson, Jackson Nieuwland and Helen Rickerby. Thank you with all my heart to Pip Adam and Emma Barnes for first publishing the beautiful object that is the *Pen Pal* chapbook. Thank you to Chris Price and my 2012 MA class for the wild times. Thank you to Julie Hanify and Jo Morris. Thank you to Sam Elworthy and the AUP team. Thank you to Keely O'Shannessy for the cover design. Thank you to Sarah Jane Barnett for helping me get this Frankensteinian creation into its best editorial clothing. Thank you to *Turbine | Kapohau*, *Sport*, *Landfall*, *Food Court*, *Cordite*, *Verge*, *JAAM* and *Hue & Cry* for publishing some of these strange poems.

Thank you to Margy and Rod for buying me wonderful books as a child, and to Gerry and Lois for always being up for the best of literary chats. Thank you to Linda for playing me so many weird, moody films as a teen (especially the Chinese epics), and for being such a constant in my life. Thank you to Ina for keeping every letter I ever sent you and for always being a supporter of my writing. Thank you to my sisters Anna and Laura for being the best sisters a wee gal could ask for. Thank you to my mum for believing that my tormented primary school poetry was something worth nurturing, and for being my mum – how lucky I was. Thank you to my dad and my partner Harland for being the kindest, coolest men I know. Thank you to my daughter for being squidgy like a marshmallow, having a head the shape of a hazelnut and for nipping like a turtle.